T0199150

This Book Belongs to

_____

Answer Me

Answer Me

Developing a Heart for Prayer

Patti Greene

WESTBOW
PRESS®
A DIVISION OF THOMAS NELSON
& ZONDERVAN

WestBow Press books may be ordered through booksellers or by contacting:

WestBow Press
A Division of Thomas Nelson & Zondervan
1663 Liberty Drive
Bloomington, IN 47403
www.westbowpress.com
1 (866) 928-1240

ISBN: 978-1-5127-6045-3 (sc)
ISBN: 978-1-5127-6046-0 (hc)
ISBN: 978-1-5127-6044-6 (e)

Library of Congress Control Number: 2016917031

Print information available on the last page.

WestBow Press rev. date: 04/19/2017

Dedicated to My Wonderful Parents
Charles Londa, Sr. and "Jackie" Izzo Londa

Answer me when I call,

O God of my righteousness!

You have given me relief when I was in distress.

Be gracious to me and hear my prayer!

(Psalm 4:1)

Acknowledgments

This book came through the support, spiritual covering, and fellowship of many people. Their combined effort, commitment, and consultation have enhanced the quality of this devotional prayer journal. For that, I am so appreciative. I thank Jesus Christ for giving me the inspiration and perseverance to complete this project. I thank my husband John R. Greene for believing in me. For each book I write, he gives me the time and encouragement to complete each project. I thank Ron Shelby, an ordained minister and CPA who generously used the good old red pen on my draft for editing and theological accuracy. I thank Glory C. Odemene, author of *Fighting Monsters* and blog **SoarWithGlory.com** for taking time from her busy schedule to edit and evaluate this book from a global perspective. I thank Dianne Mize Frazier, my own personal punctuation czar and grammar queen, for perusing *Answer Me* for its final corrections. I thank **inkprince.com** for their talented expertise and artistic creativity in creating a gorgeous, coordinating cover for *Answer Me* that matches my books *Awaken Me: Growing Deeper in Bible Study and Prayer* and *Anchor Me: Laying a Foundation in Bible Study and Prayer.* I thank WestBow Press for their care and efficiency in making this book one I am proud to present to my readers. Finally, I thank my many friends and family members who supported and prayed for me throughout the entire writing process, from contract to finished book. To you, I am eternally grateful.

Table of Contents

Preface

When I was a young adult, I prayed over a major decision I needed to make. I prayed for an entire school year, asking God whether I should move from Ft. Worth, Texas, to Houston, Texas. I made a deal with God. I remember specifically telling God, "I'll read the Bible and pray until you give me an answer." It should not have been a surprise to me that I had to read the entire Bible ALL THE WAY THROUGH until I received the answer. The answer came through a verse in the New American Standard Bible which states, "Just as you do not know the path of the wind and how bones are formed in the womb of the pregnant woman, so you do not know the activity of God who makes all things." (Ecclesiastes 11:5)

Explaining how this verse told me to move to Houston is tough. However, I believe that the Holy Spirit used God's Word to answer me and I did move to Houston.

Prayer journaling has been part of my life since I was a seventeen-year-old teenager. I was prayer journaling before journaling was even popular. If you were to look in my closet, you would see 45 years of prayer journals on my upper shelf. So, it was natural when God said, "Patti, I want you to write devotional prayer journals. This is what I have been preparing you for."

I am convinced Christians need to pray daily. Therefore, I wrote this devotional prayer journal *Answer Me: Developing a Heart for Prayer* to help others learn about the essentials of prayer and more.

Introduction

Answer Me: Developing a Heart for Prayer is a 90-day undated devotional prayer journal. Its purpose is to provide glimpses and insights into the essentials of prayer including:

- Basics about the Father, Son, and Holy Spirit
- How to pray
- How God answers prayers
- How to seek God
- How to pray specifically and constantly
- How God guides us
- Praying for others; and
- Addressing a powerful God.

Each of the 90 entry pages consists of an undated dateline, a topic relating to prayer, a corresponding Bible verse, a suggested Bible reading, a daily thought, a prayer request section, a personal reflection section, and a prayer. The Bible verses used in *Answer Me* come from the trusted English Standard Version of the Bible. Most original translations of the Bible do not capitalize deity pronouns following the example from early Bible translations. The ESV and this journal follow that same format for consistency while keeping the utmost respect for all mentions of God.

Answer Me is your personal devotional. There is no right or wrong way to use this journal. Do not worry about spelling or punctuation. Just allow your thoughts and prayer requests to flow freely onto the pages.

Prayer and reading the Bible are inseparable entities. Therefore, you will notice many references to the Bible throughout this devotional. The Bible, holy Word, God's Word, the Word, and Scripture are all different names used to represent the holy book throughout *Answer Me*.

Books of the Bible

The Old Testament

Genesis	2 Chronicles	Daniel
Exodus	Ezra	Hosea
Leviticus	Nehemiah	Joel
Numbers	Esther	Amos
Deuteronomy	Job	Obadiah
Joshua	Psalms	Jonah
Judges	Proverbs	Micah
Ruth	Ecclesiastes	Nahum
1 Samuel	Song of Songs	Habakkuk
2 Samuel	Isaiah	Zephaniah
1 Kings	Jeremiah	Haggai
2 Kings	Lamentations	Zechariah
1 Chronicles	Ezekiel	Malachi

The New Testament

Matthew	Ephesians	Hebrews
Mark	Philippians	James
Luke	Colossians	1 Peter
John	1 Thessalonians	2 Peter
Acts	2 Thessalonians	1 John
Romans	1 Timothy	2 John
1 Corinthians	2 Timothy	3 John
2 Corinthians	Titus	Jude
Galatians	Philemon	Revelation

Father, Son, and Holy Spirit

The High Priestly Prayer
(John 17:1b-26)

Date: _____

Behold! Jesus' Prayer

No matter what prayers we lift up to the Lord, our triune God is the only one able to meet our needs, answer our questions, and provide safe havens for us. When we trust Jesus Christ as our Lord and Savior, our relationship with him is secure. Only then can we truly pray, be guided by the Holy Spirit, and read the Bible with an unexplainable understanding.

☐ Suggested Bible Reading: John 17:1–26 (Jesus' Prayer)

Personal Notetaking:

What Stands Out to You from Your Bible Reading Today?

_____
_____
_____

Prayer Requests:

☐ _____   ☐ _____
☐ _____   ☐ _____

What do you hope to gain from this 90-day devotional prayer journal experience?

_____
_____

Write a Personal Prayer to God.
Dear God,

_____
_____
_____

Me

In Jesus' Name. Amen.

Date: _____

God Loves You

"For God so loved the world, that he gave his only Son, that whoever believes in him should not perish but have eternal life."
(John 3:16)

☐ Read John 3: For God so Loved the World

Daily Thought:

God's nature is to love us. Most notable dignitaries would not give their lives for us, but God loves us so much that he gave his son Jesus to die on the cross for our sins. Because of this sacrifice, everybody has the opportunity to choose a full life in him both on earth and in heaven.

Prayer Requests:

☐ _____   ☐ _____
☐ _____   ☐ _____
☐ _____   ☐ _____
☐ _____   ☐ _____

Personal Reflection From Today's Devotional:

_____
_____
_____
_____

Prayer:

Most gracious God — thank you for loving me and sending your son Jesus Christ to redeem me. Wash me from iniquities and cleanse me from my sin. I accept your gift of salvation and praise you that I can understand your will through your holy Word.

In Jesus' Name. Amen.

Date: _____

God Cares for You

"Humble yourselves, therefore, under the mighty hand of God so that at the proper time he may exalt you, casting all your anxieties on him, because he cares for you."
(1 Peter 5:6–7)

☐ Read 1 Peter 5: Shepherd the Flock of God

Daily Thought:

With all the people in the world, it is hard to believe God cares for us. We are one person among billions of people. But, he is Our Father, Our Savior, and Our LORD. A sparrow cannot even fall to the ground without the Father knowing it. So how much more does God care for you?

Prayer Requests:

☐ _____   ☐ _____
☐ _____   ☐ _____
☐ _____   ☐ _____
☐ _____   ☐ _____

Personal Reflection From Today's Devotional:

_____
_____
_____
_____

Prayer:

I love you, LORD. You have searched me; and you know my past, present, and future. You know my thoughts, and you still care for me. You have knit me together in love; therefore, let me cast all my fears upon you. Give me humility as I face the situations you have placed in my journey today.

In Jesus' Name. Amen.

Date: _____

God Knows Everything

"I know your sitting down
and your going out and coming in,
and your raging against me."
(Isaiah 37:28)

☐ Read Isaiah 37:14-38: Hezekiah's Prayer; Sennacheribs Fall

Daily Thought:

God, in his infinite wisdom, knows everything about us. Some people question why we should pray if he already knows everything — including what we will request of him in prayer. We pray because our prayers are an acknowledgement of our dependence on him.

Prayer Requests:

☐ _____   ☐ _____
☐ _____   ☐ _____
☐ _____   ☐ _____
☐ _____   ☐ _____

Personal Reflection From Today's Devotional:

_____
_____
_____
_____

Prayer:

LORD, you are perfect and full of wisdom. You know everything — when I sit, when I lie down, when I glorify you, and when I decide not to. Help me in my prayer life to understand that you always want me to come into your presence for adoration, confession, thanksgiving, and prayer.

In Jesus' Name. Amen.

Date: _____

The Trinity

"But the Helper, the Holy Spirit, whom the Father will send in my name,
he will teach you all things and bring to your remembrance
all that I have said to you."
(John 14:26)

□ Read John14:15-31 Jesus Promises the Holy Spirit

Daily Thought:

The Father, the Son, and the Holy Spirit are one, but they are distinct
entities. These three make up one God. The concept is difficult to
explain. Each member of the Trinity has its own purpose. Likewise, as
in marriage, when two become one, "this mystery is great," as stated
in Ephesians 5:32.

Prayer Requests:

□ _____   □ _____
□ _____   □ _____
□ _____   □ _____
□ _____   □ _____

Personal Reflection From Today's Devotional:

_____
_____
_____
_____

Prayer:

Father, give me an understanding of the Trinity. As I pray, draw me to
your Son Jesus Christ through the power of your Holy Spirit. Foremost,
I want to imitate Jesus by honoring the Word of God and always giving
honor to you — The Father, the Son, and the Holy Spirit.

In Jesus' Name. Amen.

Date: _____

God

"The LORD descended in the cloud and stood with him there, and proclaimed the name of the LORD. The LORD passed before him and proclaimed, "The LORD, the LORD, a God merciful and gracious, slow to anger, and abounding in steadfast love and faithfulness, keeping steadfast love for thousands, forgiving iniquity and transgression and sin."
(Exodus 34:5-7a)

☐ Read Exodus 34:1-9: Moses makes New Tablets

Daily Thought:

Bountiful names of God fill pages of the holy Scriptures. He is LORD, Almighty God, Creator, Deliverer, Father, Holy One, Provider, Healer, Judge, Lawmaker, Light, Most High, Rock, Redeemer, and more. Having the right concept of God is essential for growing in our Christian life.

Prayer Requests:

☐ _____   ☐ _____
☐ _____   ☐ _____
☐ _____   ☐ _____
☐ _____   ☐ _____

Personal Reflection From Today's Devotional:

_____
_____
_____
_____

Prayer:

You are the God of Justice and the God of Truth. Give me a tender heart and a humble mind as I present my requests before you. O Faithful God, quiet my soul so I can hear you speak to me. I want to praise and bless your holy name forever.

In Jesus' Name. Amen.

Date: _____

God—Our Fortress

"Be still, and know that I am God. I will be exalted among the nations,
I will be exalted in the earth! The LORD OF HOSTS IS WITH US;
the God of Jacob is our fortress."
(Psalm 46:10–11)

☐ Read Psalm 46: God is our Fortress

Daily Thought:

A fortress is for protection against attacks. God is our fortress, our deliverer, and our strength. Trusting in God and pleading for his will to be done provides safety and protection by the power of his Holy Spirit. When we pour out our hearts to him in prayer, his power is released upon us.

Prayer Requests:

☐ _____   ☐ _____
☐ _____   ☐ _____
☐ _____   ☐ _____
☐ _____   ☐ _____

Personal Reflection From Today's Devotional:

_____
_____
_____
_____

Prayer:

God, make me ready for whatever this day might bring. I need protection from my enemies. I do not want to trust in myself or in other people; thus, I need to know you are my security. Protect me and guard my steps wherever I go today because you are my mighty fortress.

In Jesus' Name. Amen.

Date: _____

Jesus—Our Intercessor

"Jesus said to him, "I am the way, and the truth, and the life.
No one comes to the Father except through me."
(John 14:6)

☐ Read John 14:1-14: I am the Way, and the Truth, and the Life

Daily Thought:

Jesus Christ is the only Way, the only Truth and the only Life. He is the only way of salvation. He is our authority in every aspect of life including our prayer life. Jesus shows us a model for praying in "The Lord's Prayer" in Matthew 6:9-13.

Prayer Requests:

☐ _____   ☐ _____
☐ _____   ☐ _____
☐ _____   ☐ _____
☐ _____   ☐ _____

Personal Reflection From Today's Devotional:

_____
_____
_____
_____

Prayer:

As Jesus prayed, so do I. "Our Father in heaven, hallowed be your name. Your kingdom come, your will be done, on earth as it is in heaven. Give us this day our daily bread, and forgive us our debts, as we also have forgiven our debtors. And lead us not into temptations but deliver us from evil."

In Jesus' Name. Amen.

Date: _____

Holy Spirit

"These things I have spoken to you while I am still with you. But the
Helper, the Holy Spirit, whom the Father will send in my name, he will
teach you all things and bring to your remembrance all that I have said to you."
(John 14:25–26)

☐ Read John 14: 15-31: Jesus Promises the Holy Spirit

Daily Thought:

The Holy Spirit lives in the heart of all believers. Through repenting,
praying, and reading the Bible, the Holy Spirit reveals himself in
holiness, godliness, and righteousness. When we pray and read his
Word, we can depend on God showing us his will through the power
of his Holy Spirit.

Prayer Requests:

☐ _____   ☐ _____
☐ _____   ☐ _____
☐ _____   ☐ _____
☐ _____   ☐ _____

Personal Reflection From Today's Devotional:

_____
_____
_____
_____

Prayer:

The Holy Spirit is my helper. Thank you for the gift of the Holy Spirit.
Let me yield control of my life so your power will be unleashed in me
to serve and live a holy life for you. May I depend upon you to answer
all my requests in the way only you can.

In Jesus' Name. Amen.

Date: _____

Praying in the Spirit

"Praying at all times in the Spirit, with all prayer and supplication.
To that end keep alert with all perseverance,
making supplication for all the saints."
(Ephesians 6:18)

☐ Read Ephesians 6: 10-20: The Whole Armor of God

Daily Thought:

To pray in the Spirit means to pray cooperatively with God. It is the highest form of prayer and communication with God. Praying in the Spirit is not goosebumps and emotions running high. It means being led by his Spirit and praying in accordance with his will.

Prayer Requests:

☐ _____   ☐ _____
☐ _____   ☐ _____
☐ _____   ☐ _____
☐ _____   ☐ _____

Personal Reflection From Today's Devotional:

_____
_____
_____
_____

Prayer:

LORD, as I pray with the intensity of your Spirit, guide my prayers so they agree with your will. As I pray fervently, pouring out my cares as your Spirit guides me, fill me with the knowledge of your Word, so I can love and serve you.

In Jesus' Name. Amen.

Date: _____

The Bible – God's Standard in Prayer

"All Scripture is breathed out by God and profitable for teaching, for reproof, for correction, and for training in righteousness, that the man of God may be complete, equipped for every good work."
(2 Timothy 3:16–17)

☐ Read 2 Timothy 3: 10-17: All Scripture is God-Breathed

Daily Thought:

Placing utmost priority in the Bible is essential. The Bible provides a clear understanding of who God is and what he wants to do in our lives. His Word is the final authority in all matters. It is not a magical answer book to achieve our worldly desires, but it is our mechanism for knowing God.

Prayer Requests:

☐ _____   ☐ _____
☐ _____   ☐ _____
☐ _____   ☐ _____
☐ _____   ☐ _____

Personal Reflection From Today's Devotional:

_____
_____
_____
_____

Prayer:

Thank you for the Bible. Let me fully understand that through reading your Word, I will know how to make decisions based on what is holy and acceptable to you. Give me wisdom to evaluate your Word in the light of counsel and circumstances so as not to stray from your will.

In Jesus' Name. Amen.

How to Pray

God Answers Habakkuk's Prayer
(Habakkuk 3:2-16)

Date: _____

Behold! The Lord's Prayer

Jesus' disciples asked him to teach them how to pray. Jesus responds with what we call *The Lord's Prayer*. In this beautiful prayer model, Jesus tells us to give him worship and praise with thanksgiving; to submit and surrender to his will; and to pray for today's needs. We are also told to confess our sins; to forgive others; and to pray for strength not to fall into temptation.

☐ Suggested Bible Reading: Matthew 6:9–12 (The Lord's Prayer)

Personal Notetaking:

What Stands Out to You from Your Bible Reading Today?

_____
_____
_____

Prayer Requests:

☐ _____ ☐ _____
☐ _____ ☐ _____

How can you make your prayer time more effective and meaningful?

_____
_____
_____

Write a Personal Prayer to God.
Dear God,

_____
_____
_____

Me

In Jesus' Name. Amen.

Date: _____

Scriptural Basis for Prayer

"Call to me and I will answer you,
and will tell you great and hidden things that you have not known."
(Jeremiah 33:3)

☐ Read Jeremiah 33:1–13: The Lord Promises Peace

Daily Thought:

God specifically tells us to pray. The principle of 'calling on God' is mentioned multiple times in Scripture. The Bible tells us to pray explicitly and the LORD will answer our prayers and tell us great and hidden things not known.

Prayer Requests:

☐ _____ ☐ _____
☐ _____ ☐ _____
☐ _____ ☐ _____
☐ _____ ☐ _____

Personal Reflection From Today's Devotional:

_____
_____
_____
_____

Prayer:

O, LORD, let your powerful Word come upon me. Let me hear your words clearly so that I am sure it is your voice. I promise, from this day forward, I will listen to you intently so your Word, the godly counsel of your people, and your Holy Spirit will direct my path.

In Jesus' Name. Amen.

Date: _____

Framework of Prayer

"Do not be anxious about anything, but in everything by prayer and
supplication with thanksgiving let your requests be made known to God.
And the peace of God, which surpasses all understanding,
will guard your hearts and your minds in Christ Jesus."
(Philippians 4:6–7)

☐ Read Philippians 4: Exhortation, Encouragement and Prayer

Daily Thought:

Prayer consists of many aspects – praise, worship, thanksgiving,
confession, and petition. People from both the Old Testament and New
Testaments prayed. Prayer unleashes the Holy Spirit and ignites a change
in us. God's people and God's church are empowered through prayer.

Prayer Requests:

☐ _____   ☐ _____
☐ _____   ☐ _____
☐ _____   ☐ _____
☐ _____   ☐ _____

Personal Reflection From Today's Devotional:

_____
_____
_____
_____

Prayer:

Loving God, I thank you for hearing my prayers. I come to you daily to
be filled with the Bread of Life. Guard my heart, so I can be like the men
of old who prayed powerfully and consistently. As I make my requests
known to you, please take away all my anxieties and provide peace.

In Jesus' Name. Amen.

Date: _____

Called to Pray

"Moreover, as for me, far be it from me that I should sin against the LORD by
ceasing to pray for you, and I will instruct you in the good and the right way."
(1 Samuel 12:23)

☐ Read 1 Samuel 12: Samuel's Farewell Address

Daily Thought:

Believers are called to pray. God can do whatever he wants to do, but he
delights in working through our prayers. Praying takes discipline. It is our
responsibility to pray for ourselves and for the needs of others. Sometimes
we hesitate to pray because we do not believe that there will be results.

Prayer Requests:

☐ _____   ☐ _____
☐ _____   ☐ _____
☐ _____   ☐ _____
☐ _____   ☐ _____

Personal Reflection From Today's Devotional:

_____
_____
_____
_____

Prayer:

O God, may I always trust you — in good times and bad times. LORD,
as I become privy to prayer requests, I realize they are revealed for the
purpose of praying about them. I call upon your name about the needs
of others and mine. Please strengthen my soul and spirit.

In Jesus' Name. Amen.

Date: _____

How to Pray

"Our Father in heaven, hallowed be your name. Your kingdom come, your will be done, on earth as it is in heaven. Give us this day our daily bread, and forgive us our debts, as we also have forgiven our debtors. And lead us not into temptation, but deliver us from evil."
(Matthew 6:9–13)

☐ Read Luke 11: 1-13: The Lord's Prayer

Daily Thought:

In prayer, acknowledge his holiness. Pray for his will. Ask him to provide for you daily. Be cleansed by asking him to forgive our sins and discretions. Forgive others. Ask him to protect us from temptations and to deliver us from evil. Pray with boldness knowing God will answer.

Prayer Requests:

☐ _____ ☐ _____
☐ _____ ☐ _____
☐ _____ ☐ _____
☐ _____ ☐ _____

Personal Reflection From Today's Devotional:

_____
_____
_____
_____

Prayer:

With thanksgiving, I call on your name. Teach me how to pray. Let me hear, understand, and feel your presence. Holy God, guard my steps; and let my requests be in line with your will. Let me do what is right in your sight, O holy God.

In Jesus' Name. Amen.

Date: _____

Just Ask

God answered Solomon, "Because this was in your heart, and you have not asked for possessions, wealth, honor, or the life of those who hate you, and have not even asked for long life, but have asked for wisdom and knowledge for yourself that you may govern my people over whom I have made you king, wisdom and knowledge are granted to you."
(2 Chronicles 1:11-12a)

☐ Read 2 Chronicles 1:7-13: Solomon Prays for Wisdom

Daily Thought:

God wants us to ask for what we need. The Bible mentions numerous things we can pray about for ourselves or for others such as, good health, God's will, wisdom, and strength. Matthew 7:11b states, "How much more will your Father who is in heaven give good things to those who ask him!"

Prayer Requests:

☐ _____ ☐ _____
☐ _____ ☐ _____
☐ _____ ☐ _____
☐ _____ ☐ _____

Personal Reflection From Today's Devotional:

_____
_____
_____
_____

Prayer:

LORD, I need to pray more. I need to pray so you can change me to be more of the person you want me to be. Remind me always that you have my best interests at heart. I need your Holy Spirit to daily direct my requests so I can pray with integrity and with great power.

In Jesus' Name. Amen.

Date: _____

Be Bold

"And when they had prayed, the place in which they were gathered together was shaken, and they were all filled with the Holy Spirit and continued to speak the word of God with boldness."
(Acts 4:31)

☐ Read Acts 4:23-31: The Believers Pray for Boldness

Daily Thought:

Be bold—not general or half-hearted in our requests to God. God wants us to be bold in our prayers. Ask the LORD for a verse to speak especially to us. Claim God's promises in prayer. We can start with John 15:7, John 15:16, and John 16:23-24.

Prayer Requests:

☐ _____   ☐ _____
☐ _____   ☐ _____
☐ _____   ☐ _____
☐ _____   ☐ _____

Personal Reflection From Today's Devotional:

_____
_____
_____
_____

Prayer:

I come boldly to the throne of grace thanking you for your answers even before you reveal them. In the power of the Father, Son, and Holy Spirit, I lift up my requests knowing that you can do all things. You will fulfill the desires of all who love you.

In Jesus' Name. Amen.

Date: _____

To Whom Should I Pray?

"But when you pray, go into your room and shut the door and pray to your Father who is in secret. And your Father who sees in secret will reward you."
(Matthew 6:6)

☐ Read Matthew 6: 1–8: Giving to the Needy; Pray to your Father

Daily Thought:

Being a triune God, we can pray to the Father, Son, or Holy Spirit because they are one. The New Testament pattern is to pray to the Father in the name of the Son by the power of the Holy Spirit. While it may be confusing to some, God knows and sees our heart as we pray.

Prayer Requests:

☐ _____   ☐ _____
☐ _____   ☐ _____
☐ _____   ☐ _____
☐ _____   ☐ _____

Personal Reflection From Today's Devotional:

_____
_____
_____
_____

Prayer:

Thank you that I can pray to the Triune God. You are my Father, my Savior, and my Counsel. As I lift up my requests to you this day, search my heart and answer me the way you deem best. I trust you in every circumstance because you are holy and to be trusted.

In Jesus' Name. Amen.

Date: _____

Praying for Miracles

"And Jesus said to him,
'If you can'! All things are possible for one who believes."
(Mark 9:23)

☐ Read Mark 9:14-29: Jesus heals a Boy with an Unclean Spirit

Daily Thought:

Miracles are supernatural feats God manifests to reveal Himself to his children. Healings, salvations, and insurmountable occurrences happen through God's divine power. Never hesitate to petition the LORD for a miracle. Many times fasting accompanies our prayers for miracles.

Prayer Requests:

☐ _____ ☐ _____
☐ _____ ☐ _____
☐ _____ ☐ _____
☐ _____ ☐ _____

Personal Reflection From Today's Devotional:

_____
_____
_____
_____

Prayer:

My miraculous God, help me! As my petitions touch heaven and I am groaning and pleading in prayer, I NEED a miracle. I cannot wait any longer. I am desperate. I fall prostrate before you and place my requests in your hands. Grant my requests and ease my pain.

　　　　In Jesus' Name. Amen.

Date: _____

Praying the Scriptures

"For the word of God is living and active, sharper than any two-edged sword, piercing to the division of soul and of spirit, of joints and of marrow, and discerning the thoughts and intentions of the heart." (Hebrews 4:12)

□ Read Hebrews 4: His Voice; Word of God

Daily Thought:

Many people have discovered the power of praying Scriptures in their communication with God. Through this method, they develop confidence in their praying. To "pray the Scriptures," try substituting names, pronouns, places, and circumstances into the phrases you read in God's Word.

Prayer Requests:

□ _____   □ _____
□ _____   □ _____
□ _____   □ _____
□ _____   □ _____

Personal Reflection From Today's Devotional:

_____

_____

_____

_____

Prayer Example from Psalm 102:1

Hear my prayer, O LORD; let my cry come to you! Do not hide your face from _____ in the day of _____ distress! Incline your ear to _____; answer _____ speedily when you are called on.

In Jesus' Name. Amen.

Date: _____

Agreeing in Prayer

"Again I say to you, if two of you agree on earth about anything they ask, it will be done for them by my Father in heaven. For where two or three are gathered in my name, there am I among them."
(Matthew 18:19-20)

☐ Read Acts 12:1-19: Peter; Earnest Prayer

Daily Thought:

Sometimes we pray with no results. This might be a time to call for others to pray with us. Jesus promises to be with us when two or more are gathered in his name. When united in prayer, God's power multiples as our prayers are uplifted and intertwined in the Holy Spirit.

Prayer Requests:

☐ _____   ☐ _____
☐ _____   ☐ _____
☐ _____   ☐ _____
☐ _____   ☐ _____

Personal Reflection From Today's Devotional:

_____
_____
_____
_____

Prayer:

O Mighty LORD, I have been praying with passion and intensity, but I haven't seen any results. Lead me to one or two others with whom I can agree and join with in prayer. Join our spirits so our prayers will reach your throne in fervency and unity.

In Jesus' Name. Amen.

Date: _____

Bible Study and Prayer

"If any of you lacks wisdom, let him ask God, who gives generously to all without reproach, and it will be given him."
(James 1:5)

☐ Read James 1: 1-26: Faith; Hearing and Doing the Word

Daily Thought:

2 Tim. 2:15 says to, "Study to show thyself approved unto God." Spending time in Bible study and prayer causes our spirits to become sensitive to his leadings. Succumbing to today's culture of liberalism is easy, but when the Word of God dwells within his people, we are less likely to be led astray.

Prayer Requests:

☐ _____   ☐ _____
☐ _____   ☐ _____
☐ _____   ☐ _____
☐ _____   ☐ _____

Personal Reflection From Today's Devotional:

_____
_____
_____
_____

Prayer:

LORD, answer and deliver today. You know my prayer requests O LORD. Consistently renew my mind, so I may know your will and obey it. Holy Spirit, speak to my heart. Remind me that with your wisdom and power, I can receive answers for peace and protection.

In Jesus' Name. Amen.

Date: _____

Who Can Know the Will of God

"Let those of us who are mature think this way, and if in anything you
think otherwise, God will reveal that also to you.
Only let us hold true to what we have attained."
(Philippians 3:15-16)

☐ Read Philippians 3: Righteousness; Straining toward the Goal

Daily Thought:

All who have repented of their sins and trusted in Christ have what is
required to know God's will. However, a mature or long-standing believer
in Christ may have an advantage in discerning God's will. This is due to
exercising grace and knowledge through Bible study and prayer over time.

Prayer Requests:

☐ _____   ☐ _____
☐ _____   ☐ _____
☐ _____   ☐ _____
☐ _____   ☐ _____

Personal Reflection From Today's Devotional:

_____
_____
_____
_____

Prayer:

Heavenly Father, make known your will to me. I am weak in spirit and
young in years. I recognize my need for you. Even if your will means I
stay where I am or do what I am already doing, give me confidence to
know that I am in your will.

In Jesus' Name. Amen.

Date: _____

How to Know God's Will

"By faith, Abraham obeyed when he was called to go out to a place
that he was to receive an inheritance.
And he went out, not knowing where he was going."
(Hebrews 11:8)

☐ Read Psalm 143: My Soul Thirsts for You

Daily Thought:

While there is no set procedure for knowing God's will, his will never
contradicts what his Word says. With Biblical guidance, prayer, counsel
of mature believers, faith, glimpses from the Holy Spirit, and sometimes
miraculous intervention, revelation of his will is possible.

Prayer Requests:

☐ _____   ☐ _____
☐ _____   ☐ _____
☐ _____   ☐ _____
☐ _____   ☐ _____

Personal Reflection From Today's Devotional:

_____
_____
_____
_____

Prayer:

LORD Jesus, it is hard to know whether my thoughts are your thoughts.
I want to be patient, but I also want to seize the opportunities I think
you might be providing. Let me understand that as I move forward in
faith that you will steer me in the right direction.

In Jesus' Name. Amen.

Date: _____

Divine Providence

"The LORD has established his throne in the heavens,
and his kingdom rules over all."
(Psalm 103:19)

☐ Read Psalm 103: Bless the Lord, O My Soul

Daily Thought:

The universe is not governed by fate. God is in control of every occurrence in the universe. All that happens is because it is either his will or he allowed it. Because God is involved in everything in the world, who better is able to answer our prayers than he who sees the big picture unfolding in our lives?

Prayer Requests:

☐ _____   ☐ _____
☐ _____   ☐ _____
☐ _____   ☐ _____
☐ _____   ☐ _____

Personal Reflection From Today's Devotional:

_____
_____
_____
_____

Prayer:

How divine are your ways, O God. Today let me see you work in my circumstances. Because everything is yours, give me a peace that you know the big picture of my life. Let me desire your will above my own. I want to seek you so I might live.

In Jesus' Name. Amen.

Call on God

Jonah's Prayer of Thanksgiving
(Jonah 2:2-9)

Date: _____

Behold! Jonah's Prayer

Many people assume they should not bother God with trivial concerns. They reserve their prayers only when there is something big. Calling on God when we are in crisis is important. But, calling on God even when we encounter frustrations, needs, or nagging doubts is also important. When we call on God daily, we gain his strength, his protection, and his comfort.

☐ Suggested Bible Reading: Jonah 2:1–9 (Jonah's Prayer)

Personal Notetaking:

What Stands Out to You from Your Bible Reading Today?

_____
_____
_____

Prayer Requests:

☐ _____ ☐ _____
☐ _____ ☐ _____

What prevents you from earnestly calling on God about a matter?

_____
_____
_____

Write a Personal Prayer to God.
Dear God,

_____
_____
_____

Me

In Jesus' Name. Amen.

Date: _____

God Hears Your Prayers

"Let your ear be attentive and your eyes open, to hear the prayer of your servant that I now pray before you day and night for the people of Israel your servants, confessing the sins of the people of Israel, which we have sinned against you. Even I and my father's house have sinned."
(Nehemiah 1:6)

☐ Read Nehemiah 1: Nehemiah's Prayer

Daily Thought:

God hears every verbal prayer, every silent prayer, every thought, every meditation, and every worship prayer. As Proverbs 15:29 says, "He hears the prayers of the righteous." He answers prayers from all who have trusted him and have a relationship with him.

Prayer Requests:

☐ _____   ☐ _____
☐ _____   ☐ _____
☐ _____   ☐ _____
☐ _____   ☐ _____

Personal Reflection From Today's Devotional:

_____
_____
_____
_____

Prayer:

O LORD, let your ears be attentive to my prayers today. I ask you to give me spiritual success and grant mercy as I make my requests known to you. Give me confirmation that I am praying in your will and with your approval. Show me answers through your holy Word.

In Jesus' Name. Amen.

Date: _____

Blessings for Obedience

"A faithful man will abound with blessings,
but whoever hastens to be rich will not go unpunished."
(Proverbs 28:20)

☐ Read Proverbs 28: Words of Wisdom

Daily Thought:

Knowledge and obedience to the scriptures bring spiritual blessings.
By faithfully obeying the voice of the LORD, being careful to do all
his commandments, the LORD will set us high above all the nations
of the earth. (Jeremiah 28:1)

Prayer Requests:

☐ _____   ☐ _____
☐ _____   ☐ _____
☐ _____   ☐ _____
☐ _____   ☐ _____

Personal Reflection From Today's Devotional:

_____
_____
_____
_____

Prayer:

God, you know me; you are everywhere; and you are all powerful. You
shower me with blessings when I obey you. I need you to restrain me
and preserve me so I do not fall into temptation and disobey. I plead
for your blessings upon me and for those I prayed for this very day.

In Jesus' Name. Amen.

Date: _____

Call on the Lord

"In my distress I called upon the LORD;
to my God I called.
From his temple he heard my voice,
and my cry came to his ears."
(2 Samuel 22:7)

☐ Read 2 Samuel 22: David's Song of Deliverance

Daily Thought:

Calling upon the LORD is expressing a need for Him, a desire for his presence, and an expectation for his help. Prayer can be expressed in many ways—a silent voice, a tired cry, a loud groan, in prostration, or with arms open wide. No matter how we call upon God, make prayer a daily event.

Prayer Requests:

☐ _____   ☐ _____
☐ _____   ☐ _____
☐ _____   ☐ _____
☐ _____   ☐ _____

Personal Reflection From Today's Devotional:

_____
_____
_____
_____

Prayer:

Dear Jesus. I need you. I know you hear me. You know about my deep distress and stressful situations. Knowing this, I ask you to speak to me—I need to hear your voice loud and clear today. Grant me the knowledge of your truth. Guide and strengthen me by your Holy Spirit.

In Jesus' Name. Amen.

Date: _____

Conditions of Prayer

"And whatever we ask we receive from him, because we keep his commandments and do what pleases him.
Whoever keeps his commandments abides in God, and God in him. And by this we know that he abides in us, by the Spirit whom he has given us."
(1 John 3:22, 24)

☐ Read 1John 3: Children of God; Love One Another

Daily Thought:

Being a believer, loving God, and obeying his Word are major conditions for acceptable prayer. God usually doesn't show us the big picture for our lives all at once, but as he shows us step-by-step what to do, we will be victorious in our walk.

Prayer Requests:

☐ _____   ☐ _____
☐ _____   ☐ _____
☐ _____   ☐ _____
☐ _____   ☐ _____

Personal Reflection From Today's Devotional:

_____
_____
_____
_____

Prayer:

I thank you for this day LORD. Let all my actions prove that I honor you. I want to obey your commands and love you more and more each day. I depend on and reach out to you. I pray in faith. I trust my deepest innermost secrets to you.

In Jesus' Name. Amen.

Date: _____

Get Rid of Idols

"All who fashion idols are nothing, and the things they delight in do not profit. Their witnesses neither see nor know, that they may be put to shame." (Isaiah 44:9)

☐ Read Isaiah 44:9–20: Folly of Idolatry

Daily Thought:

Many of our homes are filled with idols. There are materialistic idols and idols that stem from our ego and pride. Idols comprise anything that competes with our loyalty to God. It is imperative to pray for discernment about what idols occupy our lives, i.e. bigger homes, higher pay.

Prayer Requests:

☐ _____   ☐ _____
☐ _____   ☐ _____
☐ _____   ☐ _____
☐ _____   ☐ _____

Personal Reflection From Today's Devotional:

_____
_____
_____
_____

Prayer:

LORD, as I begin this time to pray, I am ready to embrace all your Holy Spirit shares with me. Rid me of any idols. Let me understand that though I may not have statues of pagan gods in my home, there may be other items and attitudes I possess. Rid me of all idols through Jesus my LORD.

In Jesus' Name. Amen.

Date: _____

Prayer—Not Just a Wish List for God

"But seek first the kingdom of God and his righteousness, and all these things will be added to you. Therefore do not be anxious about tomorrow, for tomorrow will be anxious for itself. Sufficient for the day is its own trouble."
(Matthew 6:33–34)

☐ Read: Matthew 6:19–34: Treasures in Heaven; Anxiety

Daily Thought:

The main purpose of prayer is to get into God's presence and allow his Holy Spirit to infiltrate our minds. Prayer requests are not a list of all the material possession desired. When the mind of Christ is active in believers, our wish list becomes his wish list. Striving for his mind is commendable.

Prayer Requests:

☐ _____   ☐ _____
☐ _____   ☐ _____
☐ _____   ☐ _____
☐ _____   ☐ _____

Personal Reflection From Today's Devotional:

_____
_____
_____
_____

Prayer:

O LORD, you have seen my prayer lists and have heard my requests. It is tiring running through lists without feeling your deepening presence in my prayers. I am committing my way to you, trusting you will act. I delight knowing you know what is best for me. Change my prayers to your will.

In Jesus' Name. Amen.

Date: _____

Praying for Worldly Desires

"You desire and do not have, so you murder. You covet and cannot obtain, so you fight and quarrel. You do not have, because you do not ask. You ask and do not receive, because you ask wrongly, to spend it on your passions."
(James 4:2–3)

☐ Read James 4: Worldliness Warning; Boasting about Tomorrow

Daily Thought:

Prayer involves seeking what God wants for us. Sometimes God's desires and ours are compatible. Sometimes they are not. Motives are an important factor in deciding whether praying for a material possession is acceptable. Foremost, God wants all motives to be acceptable in his sight.

Prayer Requests:

☐ _____ ☐ _____
☐ _____ ☐ _____
☐ _____ ☐ _____
☐ _____ ☐ _____

Personal Reflection From Today's Devotional:

_____
_____
_____
_____

Prayer:

LORD Jesus. I struggle in this area daily. I want to do your will, but I also desire things of the flesh. I want my motives to be pure. Just because I can afford it may not mean you want me to have it. Take away any desire not from you. Enlighten me with insights from your Holy Spirit.

In Jesus' Name. Amen.

Date: _____

When God is Silent

"It is the LORD who goes before you. He will be with you; he will not leave you or forsake you. Do not fear or be dismayed."
(Deuteronomy 31:8)

☐ **Read Deuteronomy 31:1-8: Joshua to Succeed Moses**

Daily Thought:

God always has a purpose when he is silent. Adversities and the unknowns are all in line with his purposes. God might be waiting for a godly motivation, a more consistent prayer life, a confession, a consistent Bible reading plan, or possibly even waiting to give something so much better.

Prayer Requests:

☐ _____   ☐ _____
☐ _____   ☐ _____
☐ _____   ☐ _____
☐ _____   ☐ _____

Personal Reflection From Today's Devotional:

_____
_____
_____
_____

Prayer:

O heavenly Father, I know you hear me when I pray. I am trying to be patient waiting for an answer, but it is so hard. I cry out to you to answer me, change my prayer, check my motives, or cleanse me. Do whatever needs to be done. I need relief.

In Jesus' Name. Amen.

Date: _____

When God Says Yes

"Out of my distress I called on the LORD;
the LORD answered me and set me free."
(Psalm 118:5)

☐ Read Psalm 118: His Steadfast Love Endures Forever

Daily Thought:

We feel elated when God answers "YES" to our petitions. When that powerful "YES" is received, praise should follow. Rejoicing in who God is and giving him thanks with our whole heart brings glory to his name. Joy fills our soul when God answers, "YES."

Prayer Requests:

☐ _____   ☐ _____
☐ _____   ☐ _____
☐ _____   ☐ _____
☐ _____   ☐ _____

Personal Reflection From Today's Devotional:

_____
_____
_____
_____

Prayer:

I have cast my burdens upon you, O God. You have given ear to my plea. You have not hidden yourself. Thank you for not hiding your face from me any longer. You are my holy God. You have answered me when I have called. I am rejoicing in your power and loving kindness.

In Jesus' Name. Amen.

Date: _____

When God Says Wait or Not Yet

"Humble yourselves, therefore, under the mighty hand of God so that at the proper time he may exalt you, casting all your anxieties on him, because he cares for you."
(1 Peter 5:6-7)

☐ Read Ecclesiastes 3:1-8: A Time for Everything

Daily Thought:

When God responds "WAIT" or "NOT YET," it usually seems like a "No." When this occurs, keep praying. Be patient and trust God in faith for his perfect plan. Give God leeway to act in his timing. Spend time praying that we will recognize his "YES" when it arrives.

Prayer Requests:

☐ _____   ☐ _____
☐ _____   ☐ _____
☐ _____   ☐ _____
☐ _____   ☐ _____

Personal Reflection From Today's Devotional:

_____
_____
_____
_____

Prayer:

God, you know the request I have prayed for so long. Give me strength never to give up in your power and perfect ways. This request is in your hands. I lay it at your feet. Even though I am restless, I will wait for your timing because your timing is good and perfect.

In Jesus' Name. Amen.

Date: _____

When God Says No

"You do not have, because you do not ask. You ask and do not receive, because you ask wrongly, to spend it on your passions."
(James 4:2b–3)

☐ Read James 4:1-3: Warning Against Worldliness

Daily Thought:

When God answers "NO," it is always in our best interest. It hurts and sometimes we do not understand his response. During these times, pray for his grace and mercy to be able to continue in prayer. Many times a "NO" is God's protection for us.

Prayer Requests:

☐ _____ ☐ _____
☐ _____ ☐ _____
☐ _____ ☐ _____
☐ _____ ☐ _____

Personal Reflection From Today's Devotional:

_____
_____
_____
_____

Prayer:

LORD, I don't understand. I need _____, I want _____.
I am brokenhearted that my prayers are not being answered how I want them to be answered. Help me in my brokenness. Keep my faith and attitude strong in you. Help me to understand. I love you, LORD.

In Jesus' Name. Amen.

Date: _____

When God Whispers

"And he said, 'Go out and stand on the mount before the LORD.'" And behold, the LORD passed by, and a great and strong wind tore the mountains and broke in pieces the rocks before the LORD, but the LORD was not in the wind. And after the wind an earthquake, but the LORD was not in the earthquake. And after the earthquake a fire, but the LORD was not in the fire. And after the fire the sound of a low whisper.'" (1 Kings 19:11–12)

☐ Read 1 Kings 19:9-18: The LORD speaks to Elijah

Daily Thought:

Communicating with God involves listening to him. When resting in his presence, he will often bring to mind an answer to our prayers or a conviction to pray for someone. God often makes his guidance and directions known through the sound of his low whisper.

Prayer Requests:

☐ _____   ☐ _____
☐ _____   ☐ _____
☐ _____   ☐ _____
☐ _____   ☐ _____

Personal Reflection From Today's Devotional:

_____
_____
_____
_____

Prayer:

Thank you for continuing to support me. By your Spirit, enable me to hear the small whispers that come from you. Make me sensitive and give me power to hear you—whether through your Word or whispers. I will not harden my heart because you are my rock and my righteousness.

In Jesus' Name. Amen.

Seek God

Daniel's Prayer of Confession

(Daniel 9:3-19)

Date: _____

Behold! Daniel's Prayer

God will never leave you powerless to deal with your problems on your own. Seeking God in prayer and in his Word helps us to be sensitive to presence. We all experience moments of stress, pressure, and discomfort in our lives. When we are right with God and seek him, he is waiting to answer all our needs and questions.

☐ Suggested Bible Reading: Daniel 9:3–19 (Daniel's Prayer)

Personal Notetaking:

What Stands Out to You from Your Bible Reading Today?

_____
_____
_____

Prayer Requests:

☐ _____   ☐ _____
☐ _____   ☐ _____

List 3 major concerns you will wholeheartedly pray about for the rest of this study?

_____
_____

Write a Personal Prayer to God.
Dear God,

_____
_____
_____

Me

In Jesus' Name. Amen.

Date: _____

Desire God's Spirit

"And I will give you a new heart, and a new spirit I will put within you.
And I will remove the heart of stone from your flesh and give you a heart
of flesh. And I will put my Spirit within you, and cause you to walk
in my statutes and be careful to obey my rules."
(Ezekiel 36:26–27)

☐ Read Ezekiel 36:16–38: His Holy Name; My Spirit within You

Daily Thought:

It takes practice to reflect and hear God's spirit through Bible-reading
and praying. God speaks sometimes through a loud thunder, a special
Bible verse, a person, or a still small voice. His children may not hear
him audibly, but if sought, his voice becomes evident.

Prayer Requests:

☐ _____   ☐ _____
☐ _____   ☐ _____
☐ _____   ☐ _____
☐ _____   ☐ _____

Personal Reflection From Today's Devotional:

_____
_____
_____
_____

Prayer:

You are my comforter. As I anguish in prayer, I need a fresh revelation
of your power, love, and words. I want to grip your mighty arm. Renew
me with your Holy Spirit, so I can discern your voice from others. Let
me rejoice in the power of your Holy Spirit.

In Jesus' Name. Amen.

Date: _____

The Prayer of a Righteous Person

"Therefore, confess your sins to one another and pray for one another, that you may be healed. The prayer of a righteous person has great power as it is working. Elijah was a man with a nature like ours, and he prayed fervently that it might not rain, and for three years and six months it did not rain on the earth."
(James 5:16–17)

☐ Read James 5: Warning to the Rich; Patience; Prayer of Faith

Daily Thought:

A righteous person prays with vitality and fervency; they forgive others; they pray in the power of the Holy Spirit; and they are in close communication with God. God affirms the prayers of the righteous. When praying to the all-powerful God, never give up. He is listening.

Prayer Requests:

☐ _____   ☐ _____
☐ _____   ☐ _____
☐ _____   ☐ _____
☐ _____   ☐ _____

Personal Reflection From Today's Devotional:

_____
_____
_____
_____

Prayer:

Faithful God, in the name of Jesus, make me a righteous person in your eyes. Let me live a blameless life. Let me speak your truths from my heart. Let me refuse to do evil to others. Let me be totally committed to the Word of God, so I can delight in your presence. Thank you for loving me.

In Jesus' Name. Amen.

Date: _____

Sinner's Prayer

"But the tax collector, standing far off, would not even lift up his eyes to heaven, but beat his breast, saying, 'God, be merciful to me, a sinner!'"
(Luke 18:13)

☐ Read Luke 18:9–34: Pharisee and the Tax Collector; Rich Ruler

Daily Thought:

Gaining something that is important or valuable through an inheritance is a blessing. The most important inheritance available is when one inherits eternal life. When we humble ourselves, confess our sins, and believe in Jesus Christ, we inherit the biggest blessings of all—eternal life, here and in the afterlife.

Prayer Requests:

☐ _____ ☐ _____
☐ _____ ☐ _____
☐ _____ ☐ _____
☐ _____ ☐ _____

Personal Reflection From Today's Devotional:

_____
_____
_____
_____

Prayer:

My soul was once lost, but when I prayed and confessed my sins, you heard my prayer. Thank you for who I am today. Let your Holy Spirit surround my family and friends, so they will understand that your mercies are everlasting and your truth endures forever.

In Jesus' Name. Amen.

Date: _____

Confession of Sin

"Search me, O God, and know my heart!
Try me and know my thoughts!
And see if there be any grievous way in me,
and lead me in the way everlasting!"
(Psalm 139:23–24)

☐ Read Psalm 139: Search Me, O God, and Know My Heart

Daily Thought:

Confessing sin is essential for a dynamic prayer life. In the Bible, men and women whose lives were striving toward holiness confessed their failings and sins often. Praying for the LORD to bring to light all that displeases him, including being lukewarm, leads to a closer walk with him.

Prayer Requests:

☐ _____ ☐ _____
☐ _____ ☐ _____
☐ _____ ☐ _____
☐ _____ ☐ _____

Personal Reflection From Today's Devotional:

_____
_____
_____
_____

Prayer:

O God of my salvation, thank you for being in my life. Search my heart and expose definite areas that I need to address. I ask you for insight into your mind and spirit. Cleanse me of all unrighteousness. Let me hold fast to what is good and honorable.

In Jesus' Name. Amen.

Date: _____

God's Presence in Prayer

"Whom have I in heaven but you?
And there is nothing on earth that I desire besides you.
But for me it is good to be near God; I have made the Lord GOD MY
REFUGE, that I may tell of all your works."
(Psalm 73:25, 28)

☐ Read Psalm 73: God is My Strength and Portion Forever

Daily Thought:

Following the path God has planned for us to follow is priceless. God cares for and loves us unconditionally. The more time spent in his presence, in meditation, and in prayer leads to revelation and understanding of his Word.

Prayer Requests:

☐ _____   ☐ _____
☐ _____   ☐ _____
☐ _____   ☐ _____
☐ _____   ☐ _____

Personal Reflection From Today's Devotional:

_____
_____
_____
_____

Prayer:

LORD, I open up my heart and soul to you today. I admit I am limited in my knowledge of you, but I know you have promised to take care of me and hear my prayers. I thank you for the answer to my prayers even before I verbalize them. I love you.

In Jesus' Name. Amen.

Date: _____

A Life of Prayer

"Rejoice always, pray without ceasing, give thanks in all circumstances;
for this is the will of God in Christ Jesus for you."
(1 Thessalonians 5:16–18)

☐ Read 1 Thessalonians 5: The Day of the Lord

Daily Thought:

To have a fulfilling life of prayer, living for the Kingdom of God is essential. When we live for Christ, our trust deepens and our faith becomes solid. Praying without ceasing does not mean to always be in prayer: It means to be in an attitude of prayer and an awareness of God at all times.

Prayer Requests:

☐ _____ ☐ _____
☐ _____ ☐ _____
☐ _____ ☐ _____
☐ _____ ☐ _____

Personal Reflection From Today's Devotional:

_____
_____
_____
_____

Prayer:

O LORD, I want all my thoughts, my circumstances, and my actions to be set on you at all times. Make prayer a way of life for me. Let me set aside time each day to come into your presence. Thank you that no matter how many times I ask, you never tire of the same prayer over and over.

In Jesus' Name. Amen.

Date: _____

Praying in Faith

"Now faith is the assurance of things hoped for, the conviction of things not seen. For by it the people of old received their commendation. By faith we understand that the universe was created by the word of God, so that what is seen was not made out of things that are visible."
(Hebrews 11:1–3)

☐ Read Hebrews 11: By Faith

Daily Thought:

Praying in faith brings an unshakable confidence that God knows exactly what He is doing. With faith, believers can say to a mountain, "Move from here to there, and it will move, and nothing will be impossible for you." (Matthew 17:20)

Prayer Requests:

☐ _____   ☐ _____
☐ _____   ☐ _____
☐ _____   ☐ _____
☐ _____   ☐ _____

Personal Reflection From Today's Devotional:

_____
_____
_____
_____

Prayer:

O LORD, test my heart and my faith. I know that without faith it is impossible to please you. I am asking you today to make my union with you so strong that I will live in faith and holiness. Answer my prayers to the extent of my desired faith.

In Jesus' Name. Amen.

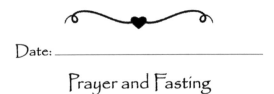

Date: _____

Prayer and Fasting

"Then I turned my face to the Lord God, seeking him by prayer and pleas for mercy with fasting and sackcloth and ashes."
(Daniel 9:3)

☐ Read Daniel 9: 1–23: Daniels Prayer; Gabriel Brings an Answer

Daily Thought:

In the Christian realm, prayer and fasting is usually a desperate cry and hunger for God. Fasting allows us to focus fully on the LORD for a breakthrough. Many experience miracles such as divine guidance, healing, or spiritual insight through prayer and fasting.

Prayer Requests:

☐ _____   ☐ _____
☐ _____   ☐ _____
☐ _____   ☐ _____
☐ _____   ☐ _____

Personal Reflection From Today's Devotional:

_____
_____
_____
_____

Prayer:

LORD, I want to gaze into heaven and be in your presence. Give me wisdom to know if, when, and how I should be praying and fasting. If you lead me to fast, give me clarity and godly instructions. During this sacred time, send your Holy Spirit to give me guidance and spiritual insight.

In Jesus' Name. Amen.

Pray Specifically

Hannah's Prayer for a Son
(1 Samuel 1:1-20)

Date: _____

Behold! Hannah's Prayer

At certain times in our lives, we encounter situations that require us to express deep cries, wails, and prayers to our heavenly Father. These prayers may involve our health, our family, our loneliness, and more. They also require praying specifically. When we pray specifically within God's will, we are able to see God's answers. This results in a deeper relationship with God.

☐ Suggested Bible Reading: 1 Samuel 1:1-18 (Hannah's Prayer)

Personal Notetaking:

What Stands Out to You from Your Bible Reading Today?

_____
_____
_____

Prayer Requests:

☐ _____ ☐ _____
☐ _____ ☐ _____

Have you ever experienced embarrassment, grief, or distress like Hannah? Explain.

_____
_____
_____

Write a Personal Prayer to God.

Dear God,

_____
_____
_____

Me

In Jesus' Name. Amen.

Date: _____

Pray Constantly

Rejoice in hope, be patient in tribulation, be constant in prayer. Contribute to the needs of the saints and seek to show hospitality. Bless those who persecute you; bless and do not curse them."
(Romans 12: 12–14)

☐ Read Romans 12:9–21: Marks of the True Christian

Daily Thought:

Praying constantly does not mean praying every minute of every waking moment. It has more to do with being persistent and habitual in prayer. We need to give the Lord focused attention and meet with him in prayer regularly and whenever a need or concern is brought to our minds.

Prayer Requests:

☐ _____   ☐ _____
☐ _____   ☐ _____
☐ _____   ☐ _____
☐ _____   ☐ _____

Personal Reflection From Today's Devotional:

_____
_____
_____
_____

Prayer:

Merciful God, every day let me see beauty in your nature, in my work, and in my family. I praise you for giving me the privilege of prayer. Teach me to pray constantly so that I may lift up prayers as they are brought to my attention. Let me pray with faith and humility. I seek you always.

In Jesus' Name. Amen.

Date: _____

Establish a Consistent Prayer Life

"But I cry to you for help, LORD;
in the morning my prayer comes before you."
(Psalm 88:13)

☐ Read Psalm 88: I Cry out Day and Night before You

Daily Thought:

It is so easy NOT to pray if we don't pray first thing in the morning. But whenever deciding to pray, it is important to establish a daily prayer routine. Establish a set time and find a specific place to pray. When that happens, a productive spirit-filled life will come about.

Prayer Requests:

☐ _____ ☐ _____
☐ _____ ☐ _____
☐ _____ ☐ _____
☐ _____ ☐ _____

Personal Reflection From Today's Devotional:

_____
_____
_____
_____

Prayer:

I come to you today with praise and thanksgiving in my heart. I want to honor you in all I do. I want to reach heaven and feel your presence. I have so much I need to share with you. I need time, Lord. Help me to commit to a more consistent prayer life, starting today.

In Jesus' Name. Amen.

Date: _____

God Values Us

"Are not five sparrows sold for two pennies? And not one of them is forgotten before God. Why, even the hairs of your head are all numbered. Fear not; you are of more value than many sparrows."
(Luke 12:6-7)

☐ Read Luke 12:4–12: Have no Fear; Acknowledge Christ

Daily Thought:

Since God created the world, he has valued his children. Because of his great mercy towards us, he has regenerated and renewed those who come to him by the Holy Spirit through Christ's death on the cross at Calvary. God values his creation because we are valuable and useful to him.

Prayer Requests:

☐ _____ ☐ _____
☐ _____ ☐ _____
☐ _____ ☐ _____
☐ _____ ☐ _____

Personal Reflection From Today's Devotional:

_____
_____
_____
_____

Prayer:

In my time of need, dear Jesus, your Word says you will not forget me. I place my burdens in your hands, trusting that through my prayers and my Bible reading, my petitions will reach heaven. Because you value me, let me value your servants. Change me and wrap me in your loving arms always.

In Jesus' Name. Amen.

Date: _____

God Answers

"I call upon you, for you will answer me, O God; incline
your ear to me; hear my words."
(Psalm 17:6)

☐ Read Psalm 17: In the Shadow of Your Wings

Daily Thought:

God will always answer prayers in accordance with his will—maybe
not in the way anticipated by the person praying, but in his perfect way.
When walking in his ways, we should make sure our prayer requests
are as clear-cut as possible, because he hears our prayers, but he may
change us first.

Prayer Requests:

☐ _____   ☐ _____
☐ _____   ☐ _____
☐ _____   ☐ _____
☐ _____   ☐ _____

Personal Reflection From Today's Devotional:

_____
_____
_____
_____

Prayer:

God, I am calling on you today. See my petitions; may they be worthy in
your sight. Change me so I can see everything through your holy eyes.
In my distress and in my comfort, I trust you to handle all my needs.
As you hear my requests, change them and mold them to your will.

In Jesus' Name. Amen.

Date: _____

Prayer Requests

"First of all, then, I urge that supplications, prayers, intercessions, and
thanksgivings be made for all people, for kings and all who are in high
positions, that we may lead a peaceful and quiet life,
godly and dignified in every way."
(1 Timothy 2:1–2)

☐ Read 1 Timothy 2: Pray for All People

Daily Thought:

Never think our requests or the requests of others are too small. We all
have requests and when we bring them to God, they become powerful
weapons in his hands. In John 16:24b Jesus says, "Ask, and you will
receive, that your joy may be full."

Prayer Requests:

☐ _____   ☐ _____
☐ _____   ☐ _____
☐ _____   ☐ _____
☐ _____   ☐ _____

Personal Reflection From Today's Devotional:

_____
_____
_____
_____

Prayer:

LORD, I know you are here with me today. I know prayer is beautiful,
so why am I so hesitant to pray for myself or others? Let me pray to
move mountains. I know you don't always answer my prayers as I would
like, but give me your glorious grace to accept your chosen ways.

In Jesus' Name. Amen.

Date: _____

Why Pray Specifically

"And this is the confidence that we have toward him, that if we ask anything according to his will he hears us. And if we know that he hears us in whatever we ask, we know that we have the requests that we have asked of him."
(1 John 5:14–15)

☐ Read 1 John 5: Overcoming the World; Son of God

Daily Thought:

When praying specifically, the results of those prayers create an appreciation within us for God who graciously reaches down his loving arms and hears our petitions. Approaching the LORD with specificity allows us to recognize his divine intervention and remain focused on him.

Prayer Requests:

☐ _____   ☐ _____
☐ _____   ☐ _____
☐ _____   ☐ _____
☐ _____   ☐ _____

Personal Reflection From Today's Devotional:

_____
_____
_____
_____

Prayer:

O Mighty God, I pray today. No more general praying. I am praying specifically for the requests above. I am praying with urgency. I will be looking for your specific answers. It is with your power and in your timing I am trusting for answers. Give ear to my words, O loving God.

In Jesus' Name. Amen.

Date: _____

Growing in Christ

"But grow in the grace and knowledge of our Lord and Savior Jesus Christ.
To him be the glory both now and to the day of eternity. Amen."
(2 Peter 3:18)

☐ Read 2 Peter 1:1–18: Growth in Christian Virtue

Daily Thought:

Recognizing the need to learn more about the Christian life is imperative, especially when first trusting in Jesus Christ. Learning to obey God's commands and principles and increasing our Biblical knowledge in God's Word is basic. Growth time is vital for efficient forthcoming ministries.

Prayer Requests:

☐ _____   ☐ _____
☐ _____   ☐ _____
☐ _____   ☐ _____
☐ _____   ☐ _____

Personal Reflection From Today's Devotional:

_____
_____
_____
_____

Prayer:

Jesus, give me a hunger to know more about you each day. Help me never to bypass opportunities to learn more about Biblical principles. Lead me to the discipleship training, classes, and personal growth sessions that will prepare me for the future ministries you have in store for me.

In Jesus' Name. Amen.

Date: _____

Whispering Our Requests to God

"O LORD, in distress they sought you, they poured out a whispered prayer
when your discipline was upon them.
Like a pregnant woman who writhes and cries out in her pangs
when she is near to giving birth,
so were we because of you, O LORD."
(Isaiah 26:16–17)

☐ Read Isaiah 26: You Keep Him in Perfect Peace

Daily Thought:

Our hearts may be quiet as prayer requests are voiced and lifted up to
our LORD and Savior. Jesus Christ conveys our whispers to the throne
of our heavenly Father. Yield to the power of the Holy Spirit; listen
carefully for his whispers back to us.

Prayer Requests:

☐ _____   ☐ _____
☐ _____   ☐ _____
☐ _____   ☐ _____
☐ _____   ☐ _____

Personal Reflection From Today's Devotional:

_____
_____
_____
_____

Prayer:

Prayer is not something I have to do. Thank you that I "get to" pray.
God, your ways are so great. You are so near that I do not need to be
anxious. I need to get my eyes away from myself and set them on you
when I pray. Help me and remind me of that today as I whisper my
requests to you.

In Jesus' Name. Amen.

Date: _____

Why God Answers Prayer

"Whatever you ask in my name, this I will do,
that the Father may be glorified in the Son.
If you ask me anything in my name, I will do it."
(John 14:13–14)

☐ Read John 14: I am The Way; The Holy Spirit

Daily Thought:

Petitioning the LORD in the holy name of Jesus and faithfully bringing our requests to him brings glory to the Father through his Son. When our motives are in alignment with his Word, he delights in responding with our best interest in mind.

Prayer Requests:

☐ _____   ☐ _____
☐ _____   ☐ _____
☐ _____   ☐ _____
☐ _____   ☐ _____

Personal Reflection From Today's Devotional:

_____
_____
_____
_____

Prayer:

LORD, let my purposes be your purposes. I pour out my heart in praise—giving you glory no matter what is the outcome of my prayer. Change my prayers to be your prayers. I know you always know what is best for me, and you see the big picture of my life even when I am unable to.

In Jesus' Name. Amen.

Date: _____

Don't Ask for Prayer Then Reject Advice

"Because I have called and you refused to listen,
have stretched out my hand and no one has heeded,
because you have ignored all my counsel and would have none of my reproof,
I also will laugh at your calamity; I will mock when terror strikes you."
(Proverbs 1:24–26)

☐ Read Proverbs 1: Knowledge; Sinners; The Call of Wisdom

Daily Thought:

Dissensions arise when we mock God's holy instructions and directions. It is never wise to lift holy hands to the LORD, petition Him, and then reject his advice. It may be difficult to accept what God says in his Word; but by living shamelessly in obedience in all he commands, we grow in wisdom.

Prayer Requests:

☐ _____   ☐ _____
☐ _____   ☐ _____
☐ _____   ☐ _____
☐ _____   ☐ _____

Personal Reflection From Today's Devotional:

_____
_____
_____
_____

Prayer:

Let me hear the words you speak. You have given me the Bible in which wisdom may be found. You have given me examples from Jesus. You have given me your Holy Spirit to guide and protect me. I plead for strength and courage to accept and act on all you counsel me to do or be.

In Jesus' Name. Amen.

Date: _____

Bearing One Another's Burdens

"Bear one another's burdens, and so fulfill the law of Christ."
(Galatians 6:2)

☐ Read Galatians 6: Bear One Another's Burdens

Daily Thought:

When encountering a sudden or strong prayer burden, wisdom bids us to stop what is currently on hand in order to pray and concentrate on what is imminent. Praying for someone may make the difference between life and death. Pray until the burden ceases to exist in your heart.

Prayer Requests:

☐ _____   ☐ _____
☐ _____   ☐ _____
☐ _____   ☐ _____
☐ _____   ☐ _____

Personal Reflection From Today's Devotional:

_____

_____

_____

_____

Prayer:

O God, I am living today to serve you. A prayer burden is upon my heart. I am praying for broken hearts to heal, for disappointments to fade, and for suffering to stop. I hurt—I am unable to do anything else but pray. You are God. Please grant rest and peace to all involved.

In Jesus' Name. Amen.

Date: _____

Praying for the Sick

"Is anyone among you sick? Let him call for the elders of the church, and let them pray over him, anointing him with oil in the name of the Lord. And the prayer of faith will save the one who is sick, and the Lord will raise him up. And if he has committed sins, he will be forgiven."
(James 5:14-15)

☐ Read James 5: Warning to the Rich, Patience in Suffering; Faith

Daily Thought:

Sickness happens due to disease, accidents, old age, or sin. It may occur over time or unexpectedly. When we pray in faith for healing and leave the results to the Lord, we acknowledge that the answers are in the arms of God. Our prayers should always be for full soul restoration in Jesus Christ.

Prayer Requests:

☐ _____   ☐ _____
☐ _____   ☐ _____
☐ _____   ☐ _____
☐ _____   ☐ _____

Personal Reflection From Today's Devotional:

_____
_____
_____
_____

Prayer:

God of Justice, you know who is sick. I do not understand why anyone has to suffer and be in pain. I need your understanding. Allow me to look at the illnesses of my friends and family through your eyes. I am praying for healing for _____ rejoicing in the power of your Holy Spirit.

In Jesus' Name. Amen.

Date: _____

Miraculous Interventions

"Does he who supplies the Spirit to you and works miracles among you do so by works of the law, or by hearing with faith—just as Abraham 'believed God, and it was counted to him as righteousness'"?
(Galatians 3:5–6)

☐ Read Galatians 3:1–14: By Faith

Daily Thought:

Miracles are divine interventions from God. God can do more than we can imagine in impossible situations because he is powerful. Miracles occurred throughout the Bible—God opened up the Red Sea; and later over five thousand were fed from five loaves of bread and two fish.

Prayer Requests:

☐ _____ ☐ _____
☐ _____ ☐ _____
☐ _____ ☐ _____
☐ _____ ☐ _____

Personal Reflection From Today's Devotional:

_____
_____
_____
_____

Prayer:

LORD, in your blessed name, I know you are the healer and the God of miracles. You rescued Daniel from the lions' den. You healed a man of leprosy. You raised Jesus to life three days after his death and burial. If you can do these miracles, I know you can help me.

In Jesus' Name. Amen.

Date: _____

God's Answers Will Never Contradict the Bible

"Every word of God proves true;
he is a shield to those who take refuge in him.
Do not add to his words,
lest he rebuke you and you be found a liar."
(Proverbs 30:5–6)

☐ Read Proverbs 30: The Words of Agur; Wisdom

Daily Thought:

The Bible is the most blessed book anyone can own. It is our instruction book for how to live a godly life. Searching the Word is critical for living a life honorable to God. God will never answer contrary to the Bible, even though Satan attempts to undermine the power of his holy Scripture.

Prayer Requests:

☐ _____   ☐ _____
☐ _____   ☐ _____
☐ _____   ☐ _____
☐ _____   ☐ _____

Personal Reflection From Today's Devotional:

_____
_____
_____
_____

Prayer:

Your Word is upright and you are faithful to me, O LORD. As I read my Bible, please speak to me through your Word. Give me confidence that I am praying your will. Help me to understand and obey all the principles and commands in the Bible.

In Jesus' Name. Amen.

God's Guidance

David's Prayer for Guidance

(Psalm 51:1-8)

Date: _____

Behold, David's Prayer

God guides us through his holy Word. The Bible is God's gift to us showing us how and why we should live a godly life. Reflecting on what we read in the Bible or hear in a sermon means digesting his principles and discovering how to apply them in our own lives. God wants to guide us. Since God has given us his Bible, let's commit to reading all of it – Old and New Testament.

☐ Suggested Bible Reading: Psalm 51:1-19 (David's Prayer)

Personal Notetaking

What Stands Out to You from Your Bible Reading Today?

_____

_____

_____

Prayer Requests:

☐ _____ ☐ _____

☐ _____ ☐ _____

Consider starting a Bible reading plan where you read the entire Bible over time. Are you willing? Why or why not?

_____

_____

_____

Write a Personal Prayer to God.

Dear God,

_____

_____

_____

Me

In Jesus' Name. Amen.

Date: _____

Giving Thanks and Praise in Prayer

"Oh give thanks to the LORD; call upon his name;
make known his deeds among the peoples!
Oh give thanks to the LORD, for he is good;
for his steadfast love endures forever!"
(1 Chronicles 16:8, 34)

☐ Read 1 Chronicles 16:8–36: David's Song of Thanks

Daily Thought:

God loves to bless his people. Give thanks and gratitude for all the LORD has bestowed on us. Stop complaining about what you do not have. Make it a practice to praise and thank him throughout your day for everything—the blessings, the trials, and even the sufferings you have encountered.

Prayer Requests:

☐ _____   ☐ _____
☐ _____   ☐ _____
☐ _____   ☐ _____
☐ _____   ☐ _____

Personal Reflection From Today's Devotional:

_____
_____
_____
_____

Prayer:

God of Heaven, you have done so much for me. I praise you and thank you with my entire heart. Thank you for loving me, LORD. Your name is majestic in all the earth. Let me serve you in every aspect of my life through Jesus Christ my LORD.

In Jesus' Name. Amen.

Date: _____

Cleanse Me Before I Pray

"Have mercy on me, O God, according to your steadfast love;
according to your abundant mercy blot out my transgressions.
Wash me thoroughly from my iniquity, and cleanse me from my sin!"
(Psalm 51:1–2)

☐ Read Psalm 51: Create in Me a Clean Heart, O God

Daily Thought:

Every single day, we should ask God if we need forgiveness for any actions or thoughts we might have that are not pleasing to him. If anything is separating us from the Lord, the Biblical course of action is to acknowledge them and deal with them in our prayers.

Prayer Requests:

☐ _____ ☐ _____
☐ _____ ☐ _____
☐ _____ ☐ _____
☐ _____ ☐ _____

Personal Reflection From Today's Devotional:

_____
_____
_____
_____

Prayer:

LORD, thank you for never giving up on me. Forgive me for my foolish rebellion. I want you to be the authority in my life—in my family, in my work, in my desires, in my problems, and in my prayer life. Let me slow down and give you my stress and worries. I need to rest in you.

In Jesus' Name. Amen.

Date: _____

The Holy Spirit Will Teach You All Things

"But the Helper, the Holy Spirit, whom the Father will send in my name,
he will teach you all things and bring to your remembrance
all that I have said to you."
(John 14:26)

☐ Read 1 Corinthians 3:10–23: Grace of God; God's Temple

Daily Thought:

The Holy Spirit brings the Bible to life, enabling us to take the knowledge given through the Word and translate it into an accurate understanding of his will. The Spirit works hand in hand with God's Word to teach, guide, and make us instruments for him.

Prayer Requests:

☐ _____   ☐ _____
☐ _____   ☐ _____
☐ _____   ☐ _____
☐ _____   ☐ _____

Personal Reflection From Today's Devotional:

_____
_____
_____
_____

Prayer:

I praise you, LORD. You have searched me and you know me. You know my thoughts and my path and you still care for me. You have knit me together in love; therefore, let me cast all my fears upon you. Give me humility as I face the situations you have placed in my path today.

In Jesus' Name. Amen.

Date: _____

Praying for Wisdom

"If any of you lacks wisdom, let him ask God, who gives generously to all without reproach, and it will be given him. But let him ask in faith, with no doubting, for the one who doubts is like a wave of the sea that is driven and tossed by the wind."
(James 1:5-6)

☐ Read Proverbs 2: The Value of Wisdom

Daily Thought:

A wise person is nourished by the Word of God. Wisdom creates peaceful and prudent people. Embracing God in prayer, being guided by Biblical principles, and seeking knowledge are characteristics of wise people. We must pray for God to fill us with the wisdom only he can give.

Prayer Requests:

☐ _____   ☐ _____
☐ _____   ☐ _____
☐ _____   ☐ _____
☐ _____   ☐ _____

Personal Reflection From Today's Devotional:

_____
_____
_____
_____

Prayer:

Help me, LORD. I'm tired. I pray and pray. I need your wisdom to get through this. You hear my prayers; I ask for your wisdom—for your vision and your insight—to get through. I am weak, but you are strong. Let me run and not grow weary. Make me wise, so I will not faint.

In Jesus' Name. Amen.

Date: _____

Doers of the Word

"But be doers of the word, and not hearers only, deceiving yourselves.
But the one who looks into the perfect law, the law of liberty, and
perseveres, being no hearer who forgets but a doer who acts, he
will be blessed in his doing."
(James 1:22, 25

☐ Read James 1:19–27; Hearing and Doing the Word

Daily Thought:

The Word of God is a living power. The Bible and prayer go hand
in hand. Through obedience to what God says in his Word and by
executing what he leads us to do in prayer, spiritual blessings will come
upon us. Psalms 119:105 states, "Your word is a lamp to my feet and a
light to my path."

Prayer Requests:

☐ _____   ☐ _____
☐ _____   ☐ _____
☐ _____   ☐ _____
☐ _____   ☐ _____

Personal Reflection From Today's Devotional:

_____
_____
_____
_____

Prayer:

You are the potter, LORD, and I am the clay. Mold me into what you
can use and equip me to be your servant in all I do or say always. I
want to accomplish mighty things in your name. I want to be a "doer
of the word." Let me read your Word with discernment so I can work
in your service.

In Jesus' Name. Amen.

Date: _____

Fruit of the Spirit

"But the fruit of the Spirit is love, joy, peace, patience, kindness, goodness, faithfulness, gentleness, self-control; against such things there is no law."
(Galatians 5:22–23)

☐ Read Galatians 5: Christ has Set Us Free; Keep in the Spirit

Daily Thought:

The apostle Paul states nine attributes of the "Fruits of the Spirit." When we pray daily for our lives to be filled with Jesus Christ, these fruits become a natural outcome in our walk with God. Developing the fruits through our own effort is not possible. We must abide in Jesus for the fruits to manifest.

Prayer Requests:

☐ _____   ☐ _____
☐ _____   ☐ _____
☐ _____   ☐ _____
☐ _____   ☐ _____

Personal Reflection From Today's Devotional:

_____
_____
_____
_____

Prayer:

O Lord, you know what situations I will face today. You know both my needs and desires. Whatever happens, let me respond with love, joy, peace, patience, kindness, goodness, faithfulness, gentleness, and self-control so I can represent you in my words and actions.

In Jesus' Name. Amen.

Date: _____

Praying for Spiritual Gifts

"Having gifts that differ according to the grace given to us. Let us use them: if prophecy, in proportion to our faith; if service, in our serving; the one who teaches, in his teaching; the one who exhorts, in his exhortation; the one who contributes, in generosity; the one who leads with zeal."
(Romans 12:6–8)

☐ Read Romans 12:3–8: Gifts of Grace

Daily Thought:

Every believer has a unique way of serving the LORD. All Christ-followers are entrusted with one or more Gifts of the Spirit. Since it is important to know our spiritual gifts, praying for God to reveal them to us is wise. Often, through serving in various capacities, we will discover our true gift.

Prayer Requests:

☐ _____   ☐ _____
☐ _____   ☐ _____
☐ _____   ☐ _____
☐ _____   ☐ _____

Personal Reflection From Today's Devotional:

_____
_____
_____
_____

Prayer:

God, I thank you for the gifts you have given me. Help me not to covet the gifts you have given others. Show me my gifts and how to use them for your Kingdom. Give me courage to try out different ministries in my search for the gifts you have bestowed upon me.

In Jesus' Name. Amen.

Date: _____

Don't Boast about Tomorrow

"Come now, you who say, 'Today or tomorrow we will go into such and
such a town and spend a year there and trade and make a profit' — yet you
do not know what tomorrow will bring. What is your life? For you are a
mist that appears for a little time and then vanishes. Instead you ought to
say, If the Lord wills, we will live and do this or that."
(James 4:13–15)

☐ Read James 4: Warning against Worldliness; Boasting

Daily Thought:

'Not boasting about tomorrow' does not mean that we cannot make
plans. God is the only one who knows what our future holds. He is
sovereign. He does not want us to assume anything about our future. We
should instead boast in the fact God will fulfill his will for us tomorrow.

Prayer Requests:

☐ _____   ☐ _____
☐ _____   ☐ _____
☐ _____   ☐ _____
☐ _____   ☐ _____

Personal Reflection From Today's Devotional:

_____
_____
_____
_____

Prayer:

LORD, help me not to fix my mind on my plans. Let me discern your
plans for me so I will not brag in my own right. I am praying for your
guidance and protection. As I make my plans, I will follow Jesus'
example and pray, "If the LORD wills, I will do this or that."

In Jesus' Name. Amen.

Intercessory Prayer

Moses' Prayer for Israel in the Wilderness
(Exodus 32:9-14)

Date: _____

Behold! Moses' Prayer

When living in Lagos, Nigeria, I visited an extremely poor area where homes were on stilts above a lagoon. The families ride in canoes around their community. Seeing their impoverishment and living conditions conjured up deep emotions and compassion within me. Once I arrived back home in Texas, I understood that sometimes we can't do anything but intercede and pray for others.

☐ Suggested Bible Reading: Exodus 32:9–14 (Moses' Prayer)

Personal Notetaking:

What Stands Out to You from Your Bible Reading Today?

_____

_____

_____

Prayer Requests:

☐ _____ ☐ _____

☐ _____ ☐ _____

Intercessory prayer is powerful. Think about your schedule and pray for the people you might encounter today. List their names.

_____

_____

_____

Write a Personal Prayer to God.

Dear God,

_____

_____

_____

Me

In Jesus' Name. Amen.

Date: _____

Testing

"Do not be conformed to this world, but be transformed by the renewal of your mind, that by testing you may discern what is the will of God, what is good and acceptable and perfect."
(Romans 12:2)

☐ Read Romans 12: 1–8: A Living Sacrifice

Daily Thought:

Life revolves around our decisions, tests, and choices. The decisions we make in life become the cornerstone for how we live our lives. Many times the decisions and choices we make become the tests the LORD uses to examine our loyalty to the world or him.

Prayer Requests:

☐ _____ ☐ _____
☐ _____ ☐ _____
☐ _____ ☐ _____
☐ _____ ☐ _____

Personal Reflection From Today's Devotional:

_____
_____
_____
_____

Prayer:

I come into your presence O merciful God. You know my trials and tests. I pray that I can see these struggles from your perspective. I know if I can see them through your eyes, I may look upon them differently and be guided to continue my prayers as is or alter them to suit your purposes. Help me.

In Jesus' Name. Amen.

Date: _____

Falling into Temptation

"Watch and pray that you may not enter into temptation.
The spirit indeed is willing, but the flesh is weak."
(Mark 14:38)

☐ Read Mark 14: 26–42: Peter's Denial; Jesus prays in Gethsemane

Daily Thought:

Many temptations come into our life. God is a faithful God. He will not let us be tempted beyond our ability. He always provides a way of escape. Pray the temptations we encounter do not lead us to sin. But, if sin occurs, ask forgiveness immediately and move forward in God's love.

Prayer Requests:

☐ _____ ☐ _____
☐ _____ ☐ _____
☐ _____ ☐ _____
☐ _____ ☐ _____

Personal Reflection From Today's Devotional:

_____
_____
_____
_____

Prayer:

LORD, help me. I am tired and weak. Weaknesses draw me into temptation. As Isaiah 40:31 proclaims, "but they who wait for the LORD shall renew their strength. They shall run and not be weary; they shall walk and not faint." LORD, my provider, I need your strength.

In Jesus' Name. Amen.

Date: _____

Praying Away Strongholds

"For the weapons of our warfare are not of the flesh but have divine power to destroy strongholds. We destroy arguments and every lofty opinion raised against the knowledge of God, and take every thought captive to obey Christ, being ready to punish every disobedience, when your obedience is complete."
(2 Corinthians 10:4–6)

☐ Read 2 Corinthians 10: Weapons of Warfare

Daily Thought:

Satan wants to destroy us. He does not want us to accept Christ or be used for God's kingdom. Strongholds appear in the form of an obvious sin or a thought lurking in our conscious or sub-conscious mind. Satan's world is chaotic and oppressive. We should examine our spiritual health frequently.

Prayer Requests:

☐ _____   ☐ _____
☐ _____   ☐ _____
☐ _____   ☐ _____
☐ _____   ☐ _____

Personal Reflection From Today's Devotional:

_____

_____

_____

_____

Prayer:

God, my healer, I do not have the ability in my own strength to break down the bondages facing me, but you do. I am overwhelmed and over-powered by the things I do that I do not want to do. Blessed LORD, as I cry out to you day and night, please do not delay your answers.

In Jesus' Name. Amen.

Date: _____

Praying With Discernment

"For God is my witness, how I yearn for you all with the affection of Christ Jesus. And it is my prayer that your love may abound more and more, with knowledge and all discernment, so that you may approve what is excellent, and so be pure and blameless for the day of Christ."
Philippians 1:8–10

☐ Read Philippilns 1:1–11: Thanksgiving and Prayer

Daily Thought:

Some believers have the gift of discernment, but all believers can be discerning in their decisions and prayers. Discernment is the ability to tell truth from lies and/or right from wrong. Discernment involves wisdom and ability to understand the deep things of God through his Holy Spirit.

Prayer Requests:

☐ _____   ☐ _____
☐ _____   ☐ _____
☐ _____   ☐ _____
☐ _____   ☐ _____

Personal Reflection From Today's Devotional:

_____
_____
_____
_____

Prayer:

God, as I lift up my heart and soul to you, please give me a discerning spirit. Cleanse me so I can hear your words and voice. Give me wisdom as I petition you with my vast concerns. I call for your Holy Spirit's guidance so I can hear and discern your thoughts on all matters.

In Jesus' Name. Amen.

Date: _____

God Commands Us to Pray for Others

"Continue steadfastly in prayer, being watchful in it with thanksgiving. At the same time, pray also for us, that God may open to us a door for the word, to declare the mystery of Christ, on account of which I am in prison."
(Colossians 4:2–4)

☐ Read Colossians 4: Instructions from Paul

Daily Thought:

We pray for others because God's Word tells us to. In praying for others, we intercede—claiming God's best on their behalf. We do not have to be a so-called "prayer warrior" on one's behalf to reach the throne of God. Praying with fervency, love, and a dependency on God is sufficient.

Prayer Requests:

☐ _____ ☐ _____
☐ _____ ☐ _____
☐ _____ ☐ _____
☐ _____ ☐ _____

Personal Reflection From Today's Devotional:

_____
_____
_____
_____

Prayer:

LORD, let me see progress in my prayer life. It is so easy to say, "I'll pray for you," and then never pray. Let me not be casual in how I treat praying for others. Let me pray as Samuel did. "Far be it from me that I should sin by failing to pray for you." (1 Samuel 12:23) Let my love be genuine.

In Jesus' Name. Amen.

Thanksgiving and Prayer

"For this reason, because I have heard of your faith in the Lord Jesus and your love toward all the saints, I do not cease to give thanks for you, remembering you in my prayers, that the God of our Lord Jesus Christ, the Father of glory, may give you the Spirit of wisdom and of revelation in the knowledge of him."
(Ephesians 1:15–17)

☐ Read Ephesians 1:15–23: Thanksgiving and Prayer

Daily Thought:

In praying for others, we are interceding on their behalf by claiming God's sovereignty over them. We give thanks in prayer so we may be wise in the knowledge of the LORD Jesus Christ. Pray with fervency, self-denial, dependence, and thanksgiving for the needs and requests of others.

Prayer Requests:

☐ _____ ☐ _____
☐ _____ ☐ _____
☐ _____ ☐ _____
☐ _____ ☐ _____

Personal Reflection From Today's Devotional:

_____

_____

_____

_____

Prayer:

Jesus, equip me to pray mightily for _____! You know the needs of others better than I do. Protect them. Give them a clear mind. Meet their physical, mental, and spiritual needs. I pray for your authority to take over their lives in every area. Thank you for giving them peace and comfort.

In Jesus' Name. Amen.

Date: _____

Pray for Humility

"Do nothing from selfish ambition or conceit, but in humility count others
more significant than yourselves. Let each of you look not only to his own
interests, but also to the interests of others."
(Philippians 2:3–4)

☐ Read Philippians 2:1–11: Christ's Example of Humility

Daily Thought:

Humility occurs when we do not think we are better than other people.
When we value the opinion of others, go last, and help others succeed,
we become more like Jesus. Putting the needs of others before ours is
practicing humility.

Prayer Requests:

☐ _____ ☐ _____
☐ _____ ☐ _____
☐ _____ ☐ _____
☐ _____ ☐ _____

Personal Reflection From Today's Devotional:

_____
_____
_____
_____

Prayer:

LORD Jesus, you are my example in humility. Give me grace to become
more like you. Shape my heart to be more God-centered. Keep pride
away from me and give me godly motives. I pray for wisdom and
understanding so I can cultivate the virtue of humility.

In Jesus' Name. Amen.

Date: _____

Love Your Enemies

"But I say to you, love your enemies and pray for those who persecute you, so that you may be sons of your Father who is in heaven. For he makes his sun rise on the evil and on the good, and sends rain on the just and on the unjust."
(Matthew 5:44–45)

☐ Read Matthew 5:43–48: Love your Enemies

Daily Thought:

God's Word tells us to love and pray for those who persecute or mistreat us. As Jesus prayed for his enemies, we also must be careful to follow God's instructions. Our prayer should be that our enemies are bought into the Kingdom of God and into a right relationship with Jesus.

Prayer Requests:

☐ _____   ☐ _____
☐ _____   ☐ _____
☐ _____   ☐ _____
☐ _____   ☐ _____

Personal Reflection From Today's Devotional:

_____
_____
_____
_____

Prayer:

Lord, I am confused. I cry out to you to save me from the hand of my enemies, but then you ask me to pray for them. I am asking you for good judgment as I seek to see my intercessions from your viewpoint. Incline your ears to my prayers and give aid to my faith.

In Jesus' Name. Amen.

Date: _____

Loving a Prodigal

"Son, you are always with me, and all that is mine is yours. It was fitting to celebrate and be glad, for this your brother was dead, and is alive; he was lost, and is found."
(Luke 15:31–32)

☐ Read Luke 15:11–32: The Parable of the Prodigal Son

Daily Thought:

Rebellion, unfaithful spouses, runaways, and more will always be with us. When loved ones become prodigals, praying for God to open their eyes to God's truth is imperative. Prodigals need God's attention daily until the case is resolved or the concern is addressed.

Prayer Requests:

☐ _____   ☐ _____
☐ _____   ☐ _____
☐ _____   ☐ _____
☐ _____   ☐ _____

Personal Reflection From Today's Devotional:

_____
_____
_____
_____

Prayer:

Thank you for being my rock in this time of need. I offer prayers on behalf of _____. I depend on you to work through this situation. Even though I believe in the power of prayer, it is so hard. Let me face this situation knowing that with you, nothing is impossible.

In Jesus' Name. Amen.

Date: _____

Waiting on God in Prayer

"Wait for the LORD; be strong, and
let your heart take courage; wait for the LORD!"
(Psalm 27:14)

☐ Read Psalm27: The Lord is My Light and My Salvation

Daily Thought:

It is extremely difficult to wait upon God—to wait for the lost soul to come to him or to heal the child who has strayed. Even when time passes and prayers linger, he has not forgotten our prayers. Keep persevering and petitioning until God moves. Trust in his timing and wisdom.

Prayer Requests:

☐ _____   ☐ _____
☐ _____   ☐ _____
☐ _____   ☐ _____
☐ _____   ☐ _____

Personal Reflection From Today's Devotional:

_____
_____
_____
_____

Prayer:

LORD, I am going to pray and persevere in prayer as I wait for your answers. Your answer may be YES, NO, MAYBE, or WAIT. I will not give up until you show me what to do. Keep me diligent in reading your Word and let your angels protect and surround those in my prayers and myself.

In Jesus' Name. Amen.

Powerful God

Jehoshaphat's Prayer for Deliverance
(2 Chronicles 20:5-12)

Date: _____

Behold! Jehoshaphat's Prayer

When we feel powerless and don't know what to do, we must keep our eyes on God. He is mighty and powerful. When we call out to our heavenly Father in our afflictions, he always hears and saves us. Cast every anxiety on him because he cares for us.

☐ Suggested Bible Reading: 2 Chronicles 20:5–12 (Jehoshaphat's Prayer)

Personal Notetaking:

What Stands Out to You from Your Bible Reading Today?

_____
_____
_____

Prayer Requests:

☐ _____ ☐ _____
☐ _____ ☐ _____

As you conclude this study on prayer, will you continue to use some form of a prayer journal? Why or Why not?

_____
_____
_____

Write a Personal Prayer to God.

Dear God,

_____
_____
_____

Me

In Jesus' Name. Amen.

Date: _____

A Life Pleasing to God

"For God has not called us for impurity, but in holiness. Therefore
whoever disregards this, disregards not man but God,
who gives his Holy Spirit to you."
(1 Thessalonians 4:7–8)

☐ Read 1 Thessalonians 4:1–12: A Life Pleasing to God

Daily Thought:

Spiritual warfare is a battlefield involving the forces of God and
Satan—good and evil. Joining forces with Satan is a dangerous and
futile undertaking. Fighting this battle can only be accomplished in
the spiritual realm. Submitting to Christ's authority and not Satan's
authority is fundamental to living a life pleasing to God.

Prayer Requests:

☐ _____   ☐ _____
☐ _____   ☐ _____
☐ _____   ☐ _____
☐ _____   ☐ _____

Personal Reflection From Today's Devotional:

_____
_____
_____
_____

Prayer:

In the power of your Spirit and in the name of your son Jesus Christ,
let me live today in your power. Make me ever aware that prayers given
in your name are heard and powerful. Let my requests reach the throne
of God and protect me from the darts of Satan.

In Jesus' Name. Amen.

Date: _____

Pray for Governing Authorities

"Let every person be subject to the governing authorities. For there is no authority except from God, and those that exist have been instituted by God." (Romans 13:1)

☐ Read Romans 13:1–7: Submission to the Authorities

Daily Thought:

The simple Bible command to submit to governing authorities covers profound ramifications. Our prayers can change or postpone legislation. Being subject to authorities does not mean giving unquestionable authority to whatever the government says. Our first obligation is always to God.

Prayer Requests:

☐ _____   ☐ _____
☐ _____   ☐ _____
☐ _____   ☐ _____
☐ _____   ☐ _____

Personal Reflection From Today's Devotional:

_____
_____
_____
_____

Prayer:

Heavenly Father, I praise you for our leaders. I come to you boldly praying that you will lead those in authority to be led by your Spirit. May they rule with justice and commonsense. May their resolve be to follow the commands you have given in the Bible. For this I pray, O Loving God.

In Jesus' Name. Amen.

Date: _____

Pray for Those in Ministry

"Brothers, pray for us."
(1 Thessalonians 5:25)

☐ Read 1 Thessalonians 5:12–28: Respect, Rejoice, Prayer

Daily Thought:

Praying for pastors, missionaries, and ministries is a privilege. It unleashes God's power upon them. Pray faithfully for their daily needs, protection from the evil one, love for the Word, purity, right doctrine, open doors to proclaim Christ, and for God's will to be done.

Prayer Requests:

☐ _____ ☐ _____
☐ _____ ☐ _____
☐ _____ ☐ _____
☐ _____ ☐ _____

Personal Reflection From Today's Devotional:

_____

_____

_____

_____

Prayer:

God of Justice, I lift up the spiritual leaders in my church, my city, and my country. Inspire them through your Holy Spirit as they preach and apply the Bible in their lives. Fill those who are listening to hear your words as they listen.

In Jesus' Name. Amen.

Date: _____

Praying in Public

"And when you pray, you must not be like the hypocrites. For they love to stand and pray in the synagogues and at the street corners, that they may be seen by others. Truly, I say to you, they have received their reward."
(Matthew 6:5)

☐ Read 1 Kings 8:22–53: Solomon's Prayer of Dedication

Daily Thought:

Consider it a blessing when leading others in prayer. One way to avoid the anxiety about praying publicly is to pray in advance of the meetings. This is called being prayer-prepared. As we pray, remember that our prayers are to be directed to God—not others.

Prayer Requests:

☐ _____   ☐ _____
☐ _____   ☐ _____
☐ _____   ☐ _____
☐ _____   ☐ _____

Personal Reflection From Today's Devotional:

_____
_____
_____
_____

Prayer:

LORD, I pray for you to heal my nervousness and anxiety over speaking and praying in front of others. Keep my mind ever conscious that I am speaking and praying for and to you. Make me an instrument and vessel for your glory as I surrender my fear to you.

In Jesus' Name. Amen.

Date: _____

Corporate Prayer

"First of all, then, I urge that supplications, prayers, intercessions, and thanksgivings be made for all people, for kings and all who are in high positions, that we may lead a peaceful and quiet life, godly and dignified in every way. This is good, and it is pleasing in the sight of God our Savior, who desires all people to be saved and to come to the knowledge of the truth."
(1 Timothy 2:1–4)

☐ Read 1 Timothy 2: Pray for All People

Daily Thought:

Praying in a church, a fellowship, or at an event can be very powerful. Its purpose is to communicate God to the entire group through the power of the Holy Spirit. It is intended to lift up the concerns of others through supplications, prayers, intercessions, and thanksgivings.

Prayer Requests:

☐ _____   ☐ _____
☐ _____   ☐ _____
☐ _____   ☐ _____
☐ _____   ☐ _____

Personal Reflection From Today's Devotional:

_____
_____
_____
_____

Prayer:

O gracious God, when I am given the privilege of lifting prayers up to you in the company of others, allow me to represent you with power, holiness, and humbleness. I am surrendering my fear and am pleading with you to give me courage to pray and speak on your behalf.

In Jesus' Name. Amen.

Date: _____

Arrow Prayers

"I said to the king, 'Let the king live forever! Why should not my face be sad, when the city, the place of my fathers' graves, lies in ruins, and its gates have been destroyed by fire?' Then the king said to me, 'What are you requesting?' So I prayed to the God of heaven."
(Nehemiah 2:3–4)

☐ Read Nehemiah 2:1–8: Nehemiah Sent to Judah

Daily Thought:

Arrow prayers are quick prayers offered up in a moment's notice. One-second prayers, bullet prayers, and microwave prayers are other names for arrow prayers. Whenever the moment arises, lift up a short heart-felt prayer for yourself or others.

Prayer Requests:

☐ _____   ☐ _____
☐ _____   ☐ _____
☐ _____   ☐ _____
☐ _____   ☐ _____

Personal Reflection From Today's Devotional:

_____
_____
_____
_____

Prayer:

Have mercy on me, O LORD. While I am busy with the tasks of today, open my eyes to see the prayer needs of others. From the depth of my heart, I truly want to lift up prayers to you throughout the day. Let me endure in my faith and in my prayers. Make me worthy of my calling today.

　In Jesus' Name. Amen.

Notes

Notes

Notes

Notes

Notes

Notes

Subject Index

I would appreciate it if you would take a little bit of your time to leave a review on Amazon or other book review sites. Reviews are hard to come by, but they help so much in getting the word out to potential readers who may desire to learn more about foundations in Bible study and Prayer. Thank you so much.

Patti Greene

Other Books by Patti Greene

Awaken Me: Growing Deeper in Bible Study and Prayer
ISBN: 978-1490893181 (Paperback)
ISBN: 978-1490893204 (Hardback)
ASIN: B01BKS418W (Kindle)

Anchor Me: Laying a Foundation in Bible Study and Prayer
ISBN: 978-1490893174 (Paperback)
ASIN: B01BLRAYPQ (Kindle)

Printed in the United States
By Bookmasters